CHASING CATULLUS

for Robin at Simon
much love

Jo

Books by Josephine Balmer

Sappho: Poems and Fragments
  (Bloodaxe Books, 1992)
Classical Women Poets
  (Bloodaxe Books, 1996)
(ed.) *Rearranging the World: an Anthology of Literature in Translation*
  (British Centre for Literary Translation, 2001)
Catullus: Poems of Love and Hate
  (Bloodaxe Books, 2004)
Chasing Catullus: poems, translations & transgressions
  (Bloodaxe Books, 2004)

JOSEPHINE BALMER

POEMS, TRANSLATIONS & TRANSGRESSIONS

CHASING
CATULLUS

BLOODAXE BOOKS

ISBN: 1 85224 646 4

First published 2004 by
Bloodaxe Books Ltd,
Highgreen,
Tarset,
Northumberland NE48 1RP.

www.bloodaxebooks.com
For further information about Bloodaxe titles
please visit our website or write to
the above address for a catalogue.

Bloodaxe Books Ltd acknowledges
the financial assistance of
Arts Council England, North East.

Cover printing by J. Thomson Colour Printers Ltd, Glasgow.

Printed in Great Britain by
Cromwell Press Ltd, Trowbridge, Wiltshire.

This book is dedicated to the memory of
Rachel Evans
(15/9/88 – 2/8/96)
and is for Tre
who had to carry on

ACKNOWLEDGEMENTS

Some of the poems and translations collected here have previously been published in the *Independent on Sunday*, *In Other Words*, *Litmus*, *per*versions, and the Barnet Borough Arts Council Prizewinners' Anthology 1996, as well as on *Common Currency*, a Poetry Society European Poetry website. In addition, some were presented at the Scottish Writing Centre's colloquium, *Creative Writing and Translation*, Mitchell Library, Glasgow, March 2001, and as part of the *Dangerous Translations* season at the South Bank Centre, London, June 2001.

The writing of this book was assisted by the award of a South East Arts' Writers Bursary and a BBC/Arts Council Write Out Loud Award.

Thanks are also due to Ann Treneman, Jenny Bloomer, Trish Thompson and above all – as ever – to Paul Dunn.

CONTENTS

Odyssey

PREFACE

What is the relationship between translation and poetry? What makes a translation faithful? What makes a poem original? Having worked on a series of classical texts – lost, disputed, fragmented, often requiring more reconstruction than translation – I wanted to explore such questions further. The result is this collection, a journey into the border territory between poetry and translation, offering versions of classical authors interspersed with original poems, re-imagining epic literature, re-contextualising classic poems, redrawing the past like the overwriting of a palimpsest. It inhabits the no-man's-land between copy and original, familiar and unfamiliar, ancient and modern, covering a range of interpretative positions from straightforward translation to versions based on or inspired by an original, as well as what I have here called 'transgressions' – versions which shamelessly subvert a source text's original intent or meaning. These source texts, too, are wide-ranging, including not only classical literature but other English translations and poems, as well as churchyard inscriptions, newspaper articles, even estate agent's particulars, fusing the strategies of translation and 'found' poetry.

But there is more here than literary experiment. *Chasing Catullus* also represents a journey of the soul, an odyssey in three stages, with a descent into the underworld, as in Homer's epic poem, at its dark heart; a response to the death of my seven-year-old niece from liver cancer. For just as classical writers rewrote and translated ancient myth in order to express dangerous emotions – passion, fear, dissent – so classical translation can provide us with other voices, a new currency with which to say the unsayable, to give shape to horrors we might otherwise be unable to outline, describe fears we might not ever had have the courage to confront. In this context, juxtaposition proved crucial, both in the structure of the collection as a whole, as well as in individual poems; a poetic device in its own right, allowing translation and original to inform each other, tossing layer upon layer of meaning back and forth between the two. For instance, 'Cancel the Invite', a poem about my niece's funeral, is followed by a reworking of a prose passage from Plato's *Republic*, implicitly questioning the validity of any poetic response to such a tragedy. In 'Creusa', the dialogue is more explicit, not just between the Trojan hero Aeneas and his dead wife, but between Virgin's original text and my rewriting of it. My aim here was not only to blur the difference between original and translation but to make it unimportant, until the reader – or even the writer – can't distinguish between the two. Nevertheless, I have provided notes on all classical and other references at the end of the book, which offer not so much prescribed but supplementary reading for those who may wish to know more. 'Each original poem,' as Octavio Paz once wrote, 'is the translation of the unknown or absent text.' *Chasing Catullus* looks to piece those lost texts back together.

JOSEPHINE BALMER

'...the cities are down, and survivors wander
the face of the earth as pirates or beggars...'

GEORGE STEINER
Homer and the Scholars

Before

We have verses guaranteed to make readers swoon,
Calliope, comrade Muse, dancing to old tunes.
So forget vast pyramids soaring to the stars,
mansions to match Jove's halls, Olympic pools and bars,
the fretted stones of Mausolus, famous for a tomb –
none can settle death's red demand and set us free.
Fire and flood wear down masons' work, names, dates, address,
years pass, blow by blow, triumphs fade, weighed down by stress.
But not this art, words formed for all eternity,
that will not fade. A monument to stand its ground
                                    beyond death.

(Propertius. 3. 2. 15-26)

Juvenal Goes To Town

There's nothing for me in Rome:
I can't lie, can't trash a tome
I haven't read, or find art
in peering up a cow's ass;
I'll never make chief critic
or horoscope page mystic.
I'm sick of lover's dalliance
so nothing at the Palace.
I'm not versed in bugs or tricks:
it's goodbye to MI6.
I have yet to rob a bank
which counts the Treasury out;
I don't own a secret vice
(hmm, the Tory whip's no dice).
An innocent secret learnt
means no fortune to be earned;
I won't dish up guilty sex,
claim a tabloid's grubby cheques.
I can't condone perjury –
no hope, then, of a jury
I don't buy my rags designer
or eat off fine bone china
so I'm only fit for scorn,
a cause for each new platform:
'Let's wash him from street-corners!'
cries the latest vote-earner
(circus sons, grocers' daughters,
receive the highest Order –
for who isn't on the make
in this world of take, take, take?).
Meanwhile landlords skip repairs
kill us with their poisoned air.
As the rich pass in taxis,
I inch through crowds on my knees.
Should flames engulf the castle,
m'lord won't lose his marbles –
a pledge, a dodge, unpaid tax,
soon brings back each bronze or bust.

If I died on your front porch
could you identify the corpse?
While the lighted trains head home
to tables laid, News switched on,
and every bathroom's singing
as slaves scrape off the city,
I'd be begging by the Styx:
'spare some change' for that last lift.
Yet for one small room in Brent,
I could buy up most of Gwent,
trade my drooping window-box
for fields, stars, a moon-drenched copse;
somewhere steel's for plough and scythe
not chains, knuckle-dusters, knives,
a place free from drunken youths,
thugs who'll leave you one front tooth.
Till then I'll starve in garrets,
risk roaches, rats – and poets
plastered on the Underground.

WC1

this afternoon
       my separate steps
              search a city

through streets and squares
                  stone
haunted by your chisel hands

in the museum
I trace your fingertips
           ancient scars
           on Assyrian statues

the deep dark marks
        of undeciphered texts

'78 Nights

(after Cavafy)

The room was dingy, always damp and dark – but cheap,
hard to find, down the alley by the Courage pub.
From the window all you could see was the brick walk
by railway arch. But throughout that distilled summer,
voices drifted up, wind-sent from the street below –
workmen, hacks, GLC clerks in C&A suits,
flushed on gassy beer and pressure-pump wine, the short
measure triumphs of pool and darts, trivial pursuits.

And there, on that sweated, sagging, second-hand bed,
we shared one body, one soul, till your lips became
my own, rose – no, the deep brown-red of vintage wine,
the stain that lingers long after the glass is drained,
so even now – years later – as I write alone
in my High Weald house, damp and dark and deep brown-red,
I'm drunk again on that same taste, same touch, same smell,
reeling once more at the red, red lies they could tell.

Wet Weekend

(Somewhere they're still kicking around,
those sad old things...)

You pick it up gently like a bruised peach
still tempting on a market stall, leather
peeling, mounts scattered, dark seed on china
dolls and plaster figurines: inside, each
snap-shot might be ours – without the kids – each
stiff great uncle ('Bert, France, 1916')
or maiden aunt trapped by the same back screen;
we almost know them all, just out of reach
on the tip of our shared tongues. But who now
to name fat babies in lace christening gowns,
list lost dogs, tick off cousins, age each niece,
and keep the waiting dust-cart from the street?
How much? Rain shuffles round and round the shop.
Thirty quid! You drop it down. Too much cost.

Feminine Ending: to Sulpicia

Midnight in Rome, summer, the year one,
and you're going home, the party's fading fast:
you've defiled aediles, procured a procurator,
got a handful of jokes past the stern new censor,
(if not amused when you declined his parts).
Even the emperor, not noted for humour,
put your best up with – let's think – Tibullus:
all right, the man's a bore, a pain, a total ass,
but there could be worse ways to share a *floruit*:
a whole new world now, new empires to crush,
you see, you're famous, a star, fêted genius.

But empires fold, dates blur, years move on,
and you're marginalised, anthologised – just;
you've evaded Vandals, survived the Huns,
got a handful of poems past the monks and nuns,
if they still removed each *Sulpicia est*;
even academia, not noted for humour,
put your best down to – let's think – Tibullus:
all right, you know the score, the same old *caveat*:
your work can't exist, or, if it does, it's trash;
just the way of the world, survival of the fittest;
you see, your name ends in 'a' and they want 'us'.

After Titian's *Bacchus and Ariadne*

(...their hand guides the brush with more confidence.
The same for the translator...)

Already she's pointing to the stars.

She's had enough of earth-bound schemes,
of mapping out the boundless maze,
disentangling all their secret themes,
to be called faithless, traitor, tart.
So when the god leaps out into the void,
as if strength and youth can fill the gap –
could compensate for theft or lust –
she'll turn and smile and take the cup.

Beyond, the faithful, fired by frenzy,
the passion that can alter words and minds;
they wave their cymbals, each sacred point,
scatter sacrificial flesh, engrossed, spell-bound.
And dreaming deep in dust-bowl caskets,
the sense most search their lives in vain to find...

What Titian read in his Catullus
and Auerbach scraped in turn from Titian,
what Ariadne somehow always knew:
that equivalence will cancel loss,
difference fade in abstract vision;
that all form, all shape, can be reduced
to these four truths:

                         yellow

      red   green

                                           and blue.

Chasing Catullus

It's the rule of attraction, the corruption of texts,
the way his corpus tastes of skin and sweat,
that taint of decay, scent of cheated death.

But then, I've always liked them old –
parsed hearts, lost minds, redundant souls;
just enough to get me fleshing ghosts,
giving them tongue, jumping their bones.

Yet sleep with the dead and you'll wake
with the worms – stripped down, compressed,
a little accusative, slightly stressed – to find
the code you crack, the clause that breaks,
is no longer subordinate, it's now your own.

Philomela

One way or another, I'd have done it myself.

Let grief, guilt or prick-sharp shame
wear down my tongue to a bloody stump;
slit my own throat, sliced off my lips,
in case my traitor speech should shape that place again.

So now I weave my words with crimson thread,
pick out my stunted songs in sacking cords –
the music of the deaf, the music of the dead.
And my soul frays at the plan I start to trace;
homes blocked in by sex and strife and sword,
the husband dropped, wife I'll never make.

And my heart knots at the thought of kids:
they seem too soft, too sweet, too pure to stitch.

During

> *Night after night*
> *I cry blood, I sweat tears, I spit out pus.*
> *But to be a god is to have no choice,*
> *a different kind who fight a different fight:*
> *I had to wreck your home, to break your heart,*
> *commit the crime, however foul the task –*
> *you see, we feel no shame, guilt can't touch us...*
>
> *In the dark I hear it, that mocking voice.*

(Euripides, *Medea*, 790-97)

Greek Tragedy

(13/10)

In the Marsden I'm reading *Medea*
that first or maybe second week:
not enough pity, far too much fear,
hubris, yes, but no peripeteia,
a fucked-up *dea ex machina*
drips bile-streaked speeches in my ear:

forget that flesh, that blood's the same,
forget the womb, don't let it speak;
disarm the heart, pick up the knife,
prepare yourself for grief's end-game –
kill today and weep tomorrow,
no going back, the path's been shown...

But we have Dads shaved in mimesis,
mothers sharing recognition scenes,
family life – or its catharsis –
and now, on cue, your masked faces,
stepping up to address her fatal flaw,
the ones to sing out: *it shan't be so.*

Cutting the Hydra

(27/3: AM)

He said: *'It's child's play, the cradle work of Junior days,*
labours I've performed since I was little more than boy;
so if you think we can be beaten by some snake in grass,
remember, of this seething coil, you are one small part:
true, it breeds on its own death; hack away a head, any
of its many hundred necks, and two improved grow back,
evil fed on evil, foul branches of the serpent's tree
but I'm its master – and what I master I destroy.'

Afterwards he couldn't even look us in the face.
I saw him going home to his own Deianira,
tucking into cutlets, mash, one more gin with bitters,
white coat deflated on its peg, buff suit skinned and shed.

Herculean Task

(27/3: PM)

I had the job of bringing it back home
the shaft we'd pulled from the Hydra's knot,
a messenger the message had already shot.

Like something new, I tucked it on the shelf
to keep it cool, to keep it still, to keep it safe –
a nodding dog for our new gates of Hell –

then belted up, pulled down my shield, drove south
into the sun, careful not to brake too hard
in case it slipped and pierced my heart.

Birthday List

(1/6)

A red silk scarf painted with the Newlyn sun.
The shriek of gulls, the hum of stone, squeezed on one CD.
Two tiny flecks of emerald the colour of the sea.
That morning at Trenow, the week between the storms

The time before we knew a cure would never come.

De Raptu Proserpinae
(2/8: 6.47AM)

Now she came to the hills wound round and round
in grass. At first light she picked her flowers:
the earth shivered with dew, violets slaked
their new-born thirst. But as the Sun advanced
on its high noon sky, night fell like a thief
and our land trembled to the touch, trampled,
dust-blown, under four sets of cloven hooves.
Their horseman we didn't know – harbinger,
camp-follower, or even Death Himself –
but now our soft meadows bruised, rivers stopped
mid-flow, fields rusted like forgotten ploughs.
To breathe was suicide: trees drained of green,
roses shed their petals, lilies shrivelled
before our eyes. And then He turned away,
swinging round the reins like the gates of Hell
grating to a close. Night scuttled after
as the light seeped back into our black world
      – everywhere was light
            sun and sky and light –
and your small daughter nowhere to be seen.

(Claudian, 3. 231-44)

Niobe

(2/8: 7.22AM)

(after Sophocles)

Like a cloud-burst on a Penwith day
that had to come yet still startles, shocks;
think of granite veined with pale-rose quartz,
a fret of stone where the bracken's frayed
by aching, flint-pierced, moorland streams;
the bind of ivy, the prick of gorse,
hedged in with comfrey, helleborine;
sob of rain, scar of hail, snow shrinking
to sigh, the sound of words you can't say.

Titan Arum

(7/8)

That day in Kew a rare bloom opened,
new *floruit* now measured out by hour –
splayed, blooded petals, bloated shaft of brine,
a magnifying glass for home-grown stamen.

And the scent of rotten fish or rotting flesh,
enough to make close ministers confess,
to turn the milk in mothers' breasts grief-sour;
like a rubbish bin in summer-time,
pressed undertakers running on half-power.

But still they come for miles to gawp:
It was so strange, so still, so swollen,
I thought it might just get up, walk...

And gasp at its common name: 'corpse-flower'.

Undertaking
(8/8: 11.10AM)

We come in from the street through an ordinary door into what
looks like an ordinary shop. There's an office, a secretary at a desk,
the obligatory brown curtains lined with beige flock. Outside, every-
one else is flicking through papers, weighing fruit, choosing out
flowers, giving friends the nod. But in here they take your name,
consult a book, then disappear out back as if checking stock. There's
time to sort our talismans – an early photo, *Four Quartets* as holy
book, *Spirit of Eden* for the ride back. Then we're ushered through
by a woman with a face like rock, as everyone looks away, although
they should be used to this, shouldn't they, it's their job. In the
corner is a small white, oblong box, draped with gauze like a fairy-
tale crib, a piece from Miss Havisham's wedding frock. We walk
up to it slowly, trapped in some dream where you know you're
moving but still feel rooted to the spot. And when at last we get
there, we don't want to look but we have to, we have to, we just
can't stop. Afterwards they make you sit down for a moment as if
you've had an accident or just given blood. There's a chapel but
we pass it by without a second thought.

We have no prayers. We have no gods.

Cancel the Invite I

(9/8: DAY)

We said goodbye in August
just weeks before the birthday
she'd precision-planned all year:
thirteen patterned paper cups –
flowers, you know, like, here and here;
thirteen plates, thirteen bowls,
thirteen bulging take-out bags
aching to be drained, thirteen chairs
we'll never steal, the conjurer
we no longer need to enroll.

Later we stand around in teams
waiting for a word or sign to start.
We balance beer and cold, cold cuts
deftly between head and heart;
out of suffering is what we say
and now, somehow, out of mind
as alcohol, ritual, flow on, kick in.
We are storing up our grief
like fat for winter, eeking out scraps
in this slow, slow race of time:
New England…a two-seater…one less bedroom…
past Junction 7…dead end…no way through…

These are not the games we have to play.
This is not the world we were born into.

Cancel the Invite II

(9/8: NIGHT)

(from Plato, via Eliot)

If you came, if you came this way to our city,
taking the old road, the salt road, up from the harbour,
and it's early days, mid-morning, late September,
sky an upturned limpet's shell, flesh-scooped, chalk blue –
or later, maybe, at dusk in depths of winter,
the sky a pebble dropping to a shore-line pool;
and if you came, if you should slip through our gates
while our guards are down, dealing out their final hands –
Proteus back from exile to walk our boarded streets,
beggar, broken king, virgin trembling on the brink
(for we know you can change face – and heart – at will);
and if you reached, by chance, our marbled market halls
to find some unclaimed spot, set out your same old wares
we've all seen, we've all heard too many times before
(and besides could buy cheaper in our local stores),
then we'd welcome you as a stranger, as a guest,
wash your dusty feet, throw fresh garlands round your neck,
commend your art, revere your turncoat trickster's skill,
and then, because poets are forbidden here by law –
for we need doctors, surgeons, men to find the cure –
we'd show you, so politely, to the waiting door.

Set it in Stone

(13/8)

I

A new green shoot
    your strong, deep root
but still I withered on the stalk
my mother thought me flawless
my family prayed for rain
    five summers –
        and then earth again

(Egypt, *c.* 300 AD)

II

The gods are jealous of those who love

I can't touch you now, Posilla
my words are stone
    my heart a fist against grey rock

(Italy, *c.* 100 BC)

III

a seven year flowering
and now I'm going back to bud

the rose you cut for me that morning –
yellow for my seedling hair –
blooms on above my ashen head
opens, closes, with each earth-bound eye
my sun, my stars, my stretch of fire-scorched sky

(Letchworth, 1996)

Demeter in Winter

(31/10)

And my grief is hardening, blade by blade,
with the grass. This month it's the raw white card
in newsagents' blurring windows: SMALL PRAM
WANTED or GIRL'S BIKE FOR SALE, JUST OUTGROWN:
it's the stray, stiff glove spiked on garden walls,
each child-chaired car iced over on its slot
in caring supermarket parking-lots,
songs slicing out like sleet through playground bars...

Centuries on and I can wake believing
that nothing's changed, that she's still here sleeping
in the room next door. Then I have to know
again how I could lose her, cell by cell,
how she could slip away, how she could fade –
that first, uncertain fall of rain-washed snow.

In Coventry

(22/12)

Even the angels are refugees,
etched in pain between past
and present, the world they have
and the one they want but just can't reach.
And here I am, in Gethsemane,
caught between Piper's Light
and Sutherland's soul-dark shrine,
an agnostic, a confirmed apostate,
lighting candles for the freshly dead;
a press-gang pilgrim with a Janus face
whose own faith blew out years ago,
still waiting on a miracle, a sign,
I know, I'm sure, will never show.

So now, of course, along it comes:
a group of school-kids gusting in
like shattered glass or keening wind
swept up the nave in threes or fours,
each hand a bead without the wood,
the rosary scraps we used to link –
about her age at final count,
the age we sisters must've been
on that first family expedition;
in matching coats and pinafores,
shrugging off their grown-up dreams
with our strange games and jointed speech,
our own dolls-house religion.

Which when I need I can't have back
and won't believe: *To The Glory
Of God This Cathedral Burned*:
one more grudge to hold against Him –
or try the light-charged vanity of man
who'll burn it down to build it up,
thousands squandered for the spectacle,
yet from my fallen, worm's-eye view,
it's just this one death I can't take.

Still I've not come for absolution,
but to curse the hand that could make
her cells divide, multiply
and stop ours from reproducing...

I know she'll never speak to us again
but today I saw her last face
in the face of a ravaged angel. And this
is where it starts and where it ends:
grief, fear, blame – the purging flames
of loss and gain. Reconciliation.

After

Who can list, who record that night's black toll
or level out its works with measured tears?
An ancient city rushes to its doom,
so long the master, keeper of the years;
now its streets and squares were strewn with corpses,
slumped in doors and alleys, rotting where they fell,
polluting the thresholds of our temples;
conquered, conquerors, the same blood-prices –
everywhere sorrow, everywhere ruin,
pain and fear, death in its many guises,
lamentation thick as smoke above the walls...

(Virgil, *Aeneid*, 2. 361-69)

Heroics

I *Fresh Meat: a perversion of* Iliad *22*

That day he dazzled like the Dog Star on a moonless sky,
rising in the dark as summer fades – too bright for bare eyes,
a fever surging through my veins, the old, old delusion:
that yes, we must die, but not now, not yet.
                                                    The old man said
I was going to the dogs, leaving him to be butchered
by the wild curs of Greece, to lie rotting, spat at, savaged
by the very hounds who now licked crumbs from his upturned palms.
But by then I would've taken Lord Achilles in my arms,
stripped the bronze from his oiled body to whisper in his ear:
'Forget Helen. Forget your dark ships lying at anchor
in my deep seas. Forget this grey city which will haunt us
for all time; its ghosts are old already and we're too young –
far too young – to tread their ashen paths.'
                                                    But we were warriors
not lovers lying side by side in hazy summer fields,
talking out our lives as dandelion or parsley seed
drifted down in search of former flower. And I knew – I knew
he would have killed me where I stood, naked and trembling, trapped
like a woman, when I had shed the armour from my skin;
for us, after Patroclus, there could be no forgetting
and no forgiveness, no friendship, no faith, no trysts, no trust,
until we'd slaked our blood-lust, repaid with increased interest
the high-rate sorrow of love long lost...
                                                    As he raised his spear,
I saw at once the evening star caught above the coves
where I had fished as a boy, that first shaft of light falling
on the mackerel scaled and gutted in our boats, floating
down the waters like a sail unfurled from a black, black ship.
And I watched him as he scoured my skin for that one soft spot
where the flesh might best be pierced; as he found it on my neck
between jugular and wind-pipe, and then drove home the point,
leaving me just breath enough to beg for more. Although now
it was my lord who turned to me and spoke at last:
                                                    'You thought
that if you killed Patroclus you would finally be safe.

Hector, couldn't you remember that I was his shield-arm,
his spear-fist, his sword-hand, his eyes, his lips, his beating heart,
the lungs through which he still breathed? How could you forget, you fool,
that another man would be watching, waiting, in the ships,
a stronger man, a swifter man, a man who would bring you
to your knees? Or did you think you could escape the full force
of my fury? Now the dogs and crows will tear your heart out;
mine will be buried with Patroclus.'

But still I pleaded
on my life, on my knees, by all the love he had once known,
not to leave me there for the strays from the ships to savage.
And I offered him my body weighed out in bronze and gold.
'How dare you,' he snarled back, 'speak to me of barter, of love?
For if I had the strength, if I could but find the stomach,
I would slice you into pieces and feed on you myself
for the hurt you've done to me. And even if you brought me
ten times your body weight in bronze, paid bone for bone in gold,
only dogs will have the pleasure of your flesh.'

'As you wish,'
I told him as I fell. 'Since I know you too well – a heart
hammered from raw iron. But believe me, my lord, your turn,
too, will come; already the jealous gods plot against you
and death waits like a lover at the Gates. For just one cell
of mortality will suffice, dividing in secret
as you sleep, the cancer creeping through your marrow – just one
slim ankle-joint, believe me, the tiniest shard of bone,
can end it all. One small robber cell waiting in the dark
to betray you without pity, without cause...

...Achilles,
the stars will still be shining, the dark seas will turn and turn,
but not for us, as other men claim their share of the light;
our flesh won't return to the bone, this virus won't retreat.

My friend, your time will come.
And I will meet you in the ash.'

II *Star, Falling*

A death is like a birth, the matron wrote,
if you're lucky, it's quick, if not... All day
we thought of her on her shrinking journey
as she finally shed the shingled flesh
that piece by piece, week by week, had just peeled
from fragile bone – this one Achilles' heel
in her almost century of winning
all the battles, the lead shaft that had lodged
like low fog in the hollow of her throat.

Which lifts, at the last, to soul's blurred vision,
everyday epics etched on heart: salt villas
shifting in the gas-lamps, starched kitchen maids
who work like Trojans by the smoking fires,
sharp-spoked message boys, heroes in waiting,
butchers-to-be whether they want or not;
a life of nets, lines that are never crossed,
and small town shop-girl code so strict, entrenched,
one slip risks dishonour, ostracism.

But now, as ever, she craved victor's crown,
to save the hour with hard-fought breath. And when
at last they thought she'd faltered, even as
the sheet was being scraped across her face,
she still held one more hostage to the light –
let it loose like warrior's quivering spear,
a hushed star falling from the Hunter's belt;
the last rasp of the last retreating wave,
low, low, tide by a darkened seaside town.

III Creusa

Did she lose her way or just stop running,
sink down to rest, unable to trace tracks?
We don't know. We never saw her again.
I didn't think, didn't even look back,
but when all regrouped, this one was missing,
comrades, husband, son, sharing the same loss.
I went home, hoping she'd do the same, hoping;
it was seething, shuddering with Greeks like rats.
Now I shook too, frightened by the quiet
but somehow in the dusk I found courage,
called out to my wife again and again,
filling the streets with the sound of her name...

If the city was an ancient rowan
hacked by farmers' axe deep in forest,
trembling, teetering, threatening, and then
at last uprooted with thundering groan,
I was the hare in its lengthening shadow,
racing on and on, running down darkness
until, at last, the light was all but gone.
Through the gloom, ghosted, I saw Aeneas,
heard him call but it was as if, as if
he was fading fast, faint mountain echo;
tried to speak but it was as if, as if
my voice was mud, words crumbled into dust.

She told me not to grieve for what was lost:
all that had passed was the will of the gods:
we weren't meant to travel on together,
ahead I faced exile, vast seas to cross,
the joy of all things, new lands now, new loves,
fresh hopes for a future in the making –
yet begged me to cherish the son we'd shared.
Then she was gone, vanished into thin air;
three times, in vain, I tried to embrace her,
three times I sensed her wraith escaping,
like clouds dispersed or a dream on waking.

I didn't know what I might be saying.
I thought he'd put a finger to my lips
the way he did when Iulus stirred in sleep
and I saw this fever or that illness,
laughing away my terrors, as he could;
I half-hoped he'd throw his arms around me,
promise that he'd stay, always had, always would.
I watched as he took up his gods and shrine,
set his ageing father on his shoulder,
wrap our son's hand in his, in miniature,
walk towards the hills through the blackened vines.

It was then I knew I'd been left behind.

Odyssey

I *Scilly*

This time we've gone too far,
disturbed the balance of our minds.
We start to fight for spit and bar,
dodge the draft, abandon mines.

We ride the swell with dipping hearts,
cling to monoliths like masts;
we sweat spray, we speak frets,
breathe in sea, piss out wrecks.

By day our tales swim off the page,
tongues crust up with salt and blood.

At night we dream of brick and clay,
sunken lanes caked in mud

II *Glendalough*

Driving up through pain-fogged Wicklow mountains,
day after all-night weddings at Aughrim,
in that creaking, cramped coupé bought because
there were, after all, only two of us,
we're singing along – *with one star awake* –
and one eye closed, as you screech round, slam brakes,
then race over each hunched humpback bridge –
the way both Dads had done when we were kids,
squeals soaring out and stomachs left behind
as our weight pulled us down like leaden lines.
Later we'll crawl from the recluse's cave
to the cracked sky at the edge of the lake,
mist risen, our daily penance over.
For now the back seems lighter than ever.

III *Chapel Downs*

Climb the highest point; here the moor's an island,
sea swinging round like a half-plaited garland;
in between, for miles, the middle land lies low.
Find a copse close as secrets. There you must go...

The best way is the old way. By the church, park:
no time for blessings, take the opposite path
(beware of the farm-dogs: they might look docile
but break the spell and there's still wolf in the soul).
Walk by Bird-in-Hand, when the path forks, veer right;
the rain will try to force you back, tongue-sharp knife.
Scramble over a hedge-stile of boot-smoothed stones;
keep a look out now for slops, swill, half-gnawed bones.
Pick a black-rooted herb with milk-white flower:
you'll need it to guard against the place's power.
By a swineherd's sin-cursed sacrificial cell
you'll find an opening, steps to earth-sunk well
(if you want to go home don't drink its waters),
twisted thorn above, in bud with ragged prayers:
Does he love me? Will he leave me? bound in twine,
from deep down the distant grunt of rutting swine.

IV *Easter in Sancreed*

The talk is of home, own small histories,
tales we tell to shore up our shifting pasts:
old jokes, old gibes, the same old childhood roles –
the one who strayed but never seemed to go.
Mist slinks across the bay, the Mount recedes,
and in the Rowes slumped back against the lych,
we stumble on some greater, graver piece:
my great-grandparents' great-grandparents
we must have brushed past time and time again
without seeing them, without sensing us.
We sponge the splintered slab with rain-soaked moss,
scrape back ivy, chisel clinging lichen,
retrace their path from porch to font to rail
then back outside once more to waiting soil.
And in the grass at last I have to understand:
even here, even now, you're slipping from my hands.

V *Letchworth Crematorium*

                              I dug my own hole:
sword-scraped the pit, an elbow's breadth,
poured libations to the world below –
milk first, mixed with honey, then fine wine,
clear water; I sowed seeds, daily bread,
got down on my knees and begged the dead,
promised I would sacrifice it all,
pile my worldly goods on pyres, scald shrines
with entrails of my flocks, my best head –
one black sheep, two barren cows, more ewes –
whatever they wanted from my marble halls.
And then, when I'd paid my Hades dues,
I slit a throat, watched life blood flow out,
dark clouds moving across dusk-dyed skies.
Now they came from the pit on each side,
souls of the dead, souls of the dying
with heart-stop cry. And my fear was green
like creeping mould, damp, knotted, gnawing:
soldiers, battle-slain and battle-stained,
brides, bachelors, long-suffering old men
and girls, seedling shoots, fresh for mourning.

(Homer, *Odyssey*, 11. 24-43)

VI *Easter in Sancreed* (REPRISE)

What we need now is resurrection.

But this is England – Cornwall. All spells
are off. We're fresh out of milk and honey
and don't have the blood or guts entailed
for self-sacrifice, sustained invocation;
true, we have our sacred cows, the old stories,
but they can't crack such close-knit tombs, shift
lichen stretched like lovers, ivy tight as lips.

Until, of course, we find our gateway;
same names for breadth, same dates for depth,
dig down and down with sticks for sword,
spit for wine, stale crow-crusts for seed and bread,
as we raise the spirits, give them last word
(if not convinced they've had their say):
BLESSED ARE THE DEAD WHO LIVE IN THE LORD

Hell no, we'd far rather live in our damp shacks
than be landlord below for all its bone-dry rents

VII *September, Chysauster*

Corncrakes drowning out tractors,
crickets more strident than strimmer hiss;
the day is breaking down to sound –
so now, maybe, the dead might speak.

But in the courtyards of Chysauster
there's still no voice as we pass by,
nothing more than a petal-whisper
from one stubborn stem of Devil's-bit
just clinging on between the stones –
scythe-passed, star-shy, sky-streaked:
the last remaining blotted dot
of some long, long-faded 'i'.

VIII *More at Sancreed*

Fifteen years on, yet another Easter
and I'm back on sacred ground again.
I can feel their breath and bone beneath my feet,
feel I'm safe, feel I'm rooted, feel I'm home –
one down for me, for them these greying rows
whose names I've learnt, deaths I now know :
John, infant, James, seven yrs, Kate, twelve –
the insistence of pain, persistence of loss,
working its way out in mud and mould and moss.

I drop my daffs down on the grave, bells
to ring our shared song across the bay:
Hold her, cherish her, know her as your own.

IX *3, May Cottages*

Everyone has their Sirens, and this is mine.

A For Sale sign on a snaking, seaside street
dull, gull-racked afternoon in Marazion:
trad. two-bed cottage of granite construction
having beamed lounge with open fire and alcove seat,
carpeted, with concrete over cobbled floor
(N.B. when the work was done vendors can't be sure),
rarely available, glorious views, must be seen.

So back home to plan: set expenses, rates, loans
against rent from lets, tax, a holiday home –
a place to heal the heart, repair damage done –
while friends and family try to tie me down:
strange what calls you back, drags you from the mast –
not stars or sky, some high ceiling made of glass,
but the floor my grandfather sowed from weed-choked grass.

X *Return to Ithaca* (VIA CAVAFY)

(Without her, you would never have set sail.
But she has nothing left to show you now...)

I can't believe the journey holds the key,
only the arriving, the death of need:

a mother tortured by those lightning nights,
father planting out his grief to seed;
the wife whose heart unravels with the light,
each dog who's had its day: they mark your map.

And then there's the land that can hold its own,
the groves whose darkness opens like a trap;
soil you'll feed with blood, mulch with lovers' bones,
furrows ploughed then filled, the blade's twist and theft.

These dreams still coil around you in the deep,
old songs returning ten-fold with the nets.
They wait there now: rooms you'd sack at a stroke –
the one place you will pollute to possess.

XI *East Meon*

The night you finally came back I walked out,
Odysseus and Penelope after the wars.
My skies had stayed the same for years on end,
had watched us pull apart and then, base metal,
dragged you home. But now the house was ridged
against the dark – our new constellation
etched in shadow between the jaded stars;
a leaky ship for all our storms, the bridge
we couldn't burn or cross or try to mend.

Until your ghost-whisper chilled against my cheek,
your lips cracked, your words like unhealed scars:
at last, at last, my love, we're here, it's ours...

XII *May Day*

Somehow I keep finding myself back on the streets,
seduced out again by the stars' scrambled maps –
a punch-drunk warrior with no night watch to keep
and only the confused dog padding at my feet
to prove that I, too, once patrolled this patch in packs.
Still, I recognise this reluctance to go home,
the age-old why-get-back-to-face-another-fight.

Up the lane the wheelie bins stand sentinel, stiff,
guarding drives from insomniac scavenger thieves;
down the Gardens, the blossom's resolutely blown,
squandering its span to the moon's cheap trick of light,
as all the lawns now, even ours, seem freshly mown
and all the let-down petals cooling cinder, bonfire ash.
Beyond the Downs, the city's taunting with its glare,
squeezing out the dark like some dodgy, called-in loan –
the lie, the con, that it's all just waiting there
for anyone to reach, for anyone to own;
through this haze of booze, recrimination, grief,
enough tonight to make you shout or swear or weep
but not quite enough – not yet – to make it peace.

Across forty miles Crystal Palace transmitter winks,
a sense of time and space, infinity on the blink –
so beautiful, so terrifying, so fucking brief.

NOTES

George Steiner's essay 'Homer and the Scholars' is collected in *Language and Silence: Essays 1958-1966* (Faber & Faber, 1967).

Before
The Propertius translation was inspired by Ezra Pound's controversial 1919 version, 'Homage to Sextus Propertius'.

Juvenal Goes to Town (14-15): Based on Juvenal's third satire which details the deprivations of life in Rome in the early 2nd century AD.

'78 Nights (17): A version of C.P. Cavafy's 1907 poem 'One Night', which, like Cavafy himself, speaks Greek 'with a slight British accent'.

Wet Weekend (18): The dedicatory quotation is from Cavafy's 1918 poem, 'The Afternoon Sun'.

Feminine Ending: to Sulpicia (19): Scholars have often attributed the Latin poet Sulpicia's handful of surviving poems to her male contemporary Tibullus. Restored to its rightful owner in more recent years, her witty, erotic verse is the only known example of women's poetry from classical Rome.

the year one: Sulpicia was writing around the turn of the 1st century BC / 1st century AD.

Sulpicia est: 'this is Sulpicia'.

your name ends in: feminine proper nouns in Latin usually end in '-a', while their masculine counterparts end in '-us'.

After Titian's *Bacchus and Ariadne* (20): Quotation from *Critische Dichtkunst* ('Critical Poetics') by Johann Christoph Gottsched (collected and translated in *Translation/ History/ Culture: A Sourcebook*, edited by André Lefevere (Routledge, 1992). Titian's 1522 painting 'Bacchus and Ariadne' depicts the moment when the god catches sight of Ariadne on Naxos. Deserted by her lover, Theseus, after helping him to escape from the Minotaur's maze, a distraught Ariadne turns away towards a crown of stars, while Bacchus, surrounded by his orgiastic revellers, leaps down from his chariot towards her, overwhelmed by wild passion. Frank Auerbach's 1971 painting 'After Titian's Bacchus and Ariadne' reworks Titian original in abstract expressionist style, turning Titian's delicately worked characters into rigorous girders of colour.

Beyond, the faithful...: this passage, based on Catullus, 64. 254-64, was Titian's starting point for his painting.

sacred shaft: a stroke of the thyrsus, the sacred rod carried by Bacchic revellers, was said to induce ritual frenzy.

dust-bowl caskets: containing the cult's sacred serpents and other ritual paraphernalia.

Philomela (22): In Greek myth, Philomena was raped by her brother-in-law, Tereus, who cut out her tongue in order to stop her from revealing his crime. But Philomela depicted her ordeal in a tapestry which she then sent to her sister Procne. On discovering the truth about Tereus, Procne murdered their son Itys, serving his flesh up to his father at a feast. The gods later turned the sisters into birds, a swallow and a nightingale.

During

Euripides' play *Medea* centres on the eastern enchantress' abandonment by her Greek lover Jason, whom she had helped in his quest for the Golden Fleece. In revenge she determines to kill their children in their father's presence.

Greek Tragedy (24):

Marsden: The Royal Marsden Hospital, Sutton.

pity...fear: according to Aristotle, the emotions tragedy engenders in its audience.

hubris: the pride or 'fatal flaw' which contributes to a tragic hero's downfall.

peripeteia: the 'turning around' or reversal of fortune on which a tragic plot is hinged.

dea ex machina: in Greek tragic theatre, a mechanical contraption lowered down from above on to the stage, as a god came down from heaven to resolve the plot at the end of a play, hence its proverbial meaning (with the more usual masculine form *deus*) as a heaven-sent rescuer.

forget that flesh...: italic passage loosely translated from Euripides, *Medea*, 1240-49.

mimesis: or 'imitation', a term Aristotle uses of the representation of reality in drama.

recognition scenes: a common element in tragedy, helping to forward the plot.

catharsis: according to Aristotle, the purging of emotion that the conclusion of a tragic plot brings to its audience.

it shan't be so: from a line in *Medea* by the leader of the Chorus (813).

Cutting the Hydra (25): The slaying of the many-headed serpent, the Hydra, by the hero Heracles, or Hercules, gave classical Greek the expression *hudran temnein*, 'to cut the Hydra', used proverbially for attempting an impossible task.

It's child's play...: italic passage translated from Ovid, *Metamorphoses*, 9. 67-74, in which Hercules boasts about his triumph over the Hydra.

Deianira: the wife of Hercules, later tricked into killing the hero by giving him a shirt poisoned with the Hydra's blood.

buff suit: Hercules is usually depicted in Greek art wearing a lion-skin.

Herculean Task (26): After killing the Hydra, Hercules dipped his arrows in the monster's poisonous blood to make their wounds incurable.

nodding dog: Hercules' eleventh labour was to descend into the Underworld and steal Cerberus, the three-headed dog who guarded the gates of hell.

De Raptu Proserpinae (28): Claudian's unfinished epic poem of *c*. 400 AD describes how Proserpina (the Latin form of Persephone), daughter of the corn-goddess Ceres or Demeter, was abducted by Pluto, god of the Underworld.

Niobe (29): Niobe, who had seven sons and seven daughters, boasted that she was therefore superior to Leto, mother of Apollo and Artemis. When the twin gods killed all her children in punishment, Niobe's grief turned her to stone. The poem is based on a Chorus from Sophocles' tragedy *Antigone* (824-31).

Titan Arum (30): The titan arum, a giant lily native to Sumatra, and the world's largest flower, blooms once every 33 years, producing a variety of obnoxious odours to attract pollinating insects such as carrion beetles or flesh flies. In early August 1996, a Titan Arum flowered at Kew to great media interest.

It was so strange...: quotes from 'Scents Assail Sensibilities', *Daily Telegraph*, and 'So This Is What's Behind The Wrinkled Nose Epidemic', *The Independent* (both 1/8/96).

Cancel the Invite II (33): Based on Plato, *Republic*, 398a. All but the most morally stern poets were to be banned from Plato's utopian city.

If you came...: the translation was inspired by lines 21-31 of T.S. Eliot's poem 'Little Gidding' from *Four Quartets*.

Set It In Stone (34): The first two sections are based on ancient funerary inscriptions.

Demeter in Winter (35): After the abduction of her daughter (see p.28 and note above), Demeter wandered the earth in search of her, until Jupiter granted that she should be restored to her mother, provided she hadn't eaten any food in the Underworld. But as Persephone (Proserpina) had eaten six grains of a pomegranate, Jupiter ruled that she should spend six months of the year with her mother and six months in the Underworld, during which time Demeter mourned her loss, bringing winter to the earth.

In Coventry (36-37): On the night of 14 November 1940, Coventry's ancient cathedral was destroyed by German bombers. A new cathedral, designed by Sir Basil Spence, was consecrated on 25 May 1962, and has subsequently become known for its ministry of forgiveness and reconciliation.

angels...etched: John Hutton's vast glass entrance screen, engraved with angels, divides the new cathedral from the ruins of the old.

Gethsemane: the Chapel of Christ in Gethsemane, to the right of the Lady Chapel.

Piper's Light: the stained-glass Baptistery windows, designed by John Piper.

Sutherland...shrine: Graham Sutherland's altar tapestry of Christ in Glory.

After

The passage from Virgil's epic Latin poem, the *Aeneid*, describes the fall of Troy to the Greeks.

Fresh Meat (41-42): A version of *Iliad* 22 (25-360, condensed), commissioned by the journal *per*versions, and based on Homer's account of the single combat between the Greek hero Achilles and the Trojan champion Hector, as Achilles seeks to avenge his fellow-warrior and lover Patroclus, whom Hector has slain. The poem plays on the Greek's homoerotic sub-text, not just of Achilles' love for Patroclus but also the sub-conscious undercurrent of desire between the two opposing warriors, particularly in a speech by Hector, translated here (even if almost certainly a scribe's later interpolation). Drawn by Hector's ascribed words, I perverted my version with this reading, changing the distanced, third-person narrative of Homer's epic into the first-person lament of Hector's ghost.

death waits...slim ankle-joint: As a baby, Achilles had been bathed by his mother, Thetis, in the river Styx, making him immortal – except for the ankle she'd used to hold him. He was later slain at the Gates of Troy by an arrow shot into this ankle by the Trojan price Paris. Neither the story of Achilles' immortality, nor of his death, appear in Homer.

Star, Falling (43): In memoriam Vi Richards (1901-95).

Creusa (44-45): In Virgil's epic Latin poem, the *Aeneid*, Creusa, wife of the Trojan prince Aeneas, is lost during the Trojans' flight from their sacked city. When Aeneas goes back into the burning citadel to try to find her, she appears to him as a ghost, prophesising his destiny as the founder of Rome, although, like Aeneas, we never learn what her exact fate has been.

Did she lose her way....: italic passage translated from Virgil, *Aeneid*, 2. 738-45.

if the city was an ancient rowan....: comes from *Aeneid*, 2. 626-31.

she told me not to grieve...: italic passage translated from *Aeneid*, 2. 776-94 (condensed).

I watched as he took up his gods...blackened vines: based on *Aeneid*, 2. 804.
Iulus: son of Creusa and Aeneas.

Odyssey (46-57): The twelve poems in this section are inspired by Homer's epic poem, which tells of the ten-year adventures of the Greek hero Odysseus on his way home to Ithaca from Troy.

I *Scilly* (46): Based on Odysseus' encounter with the Lotus-Eaters, in whose land he and his men arrive after sailing from Troy. As Odysseus later explains: 'whoever of them ate the honey-sweet fruit of the lotus had no longer any wish to return...these men I brought back to the ship under compulsion, weeping...' (*Odyssey*, 9. 94-97).

II *Glendalough* (47): Glendalough is an ancient Irish monastic site, south of Dublin, founded by St Kevin. This poem has its roots in the Cyclops episode in the *Odyssey*; imprisoned with his men in the cave of the one-eyed giant Cyclops, Polyphemus, Odysseus and companions escape by blinding the giant and hiding under the bellies of his flock of sheep (*Odyssey*, 9. 175-542).
with one star awake: from the poem (best-known as a song) 'She Moved Through the Fair' by Padraic Colum (1881-1972).
recluse's cave: St Kevin's Bed, a cave on the site's Upper Lake, was thought to have been the hermit-saint's favourite retreat.

III *Chapel Downs* (48): Chapel Downs is an ancient Celtic site, just west of the village of Sancreed, Cornwall.
Climb the highest point...: italic passage translated from *Odyssey*, 10. 194-97: arriving on the island of Aeaea, Odysseus climbs a rock and sees a house in a clearing. When his men explore further, they find it belongs to the enchantress Circe. As they approach, they are surrounded by strangely docile wild beasts. Circe invites the men inside but, after wining and dining them, turns them into pigs.
black-rooted herb with milk-white flower: as Odysseus sets out to rescue his friends, he meets the messenger god Hermes in disguise, who advises on how to protect against Circe's spells.
a swineherd's sin-cursed sacrificial cell: according to local Cornish legend, St Credan, the founding saint of Sancreed church, was a wealthy young man who accidentally killed his father. In remorse, he became a hermit-swineherd.

IV *Easter in Sancreed* (49): This poem, as well as poems V-VIII, are all inspired by *Odyssey* XI or the 'Book of the Dead' in which Odysseus descends into the Underworld.

VI *Easter in Sancreed* (REPRISE) (51): BLESSED ARE THE DEAD...: based on the inscription on the graves of my ancestors, James and Catherine Rowe, in Sancreed churchyard.

Hell, no...: a version of *Odyssey,* 11. 489-91: meeting the ghost of Achilles, Odysseus tells him to not to grieve at being dead but to remember his glory alive. 'I would rather live as a slave on earth, a poor, landless man,' replies Achilles, 'than be lord of all the perished dead.'

VII *September, Chysauster* (52): Chysauster is an Iron Age village in west Cornwall.

Devil's-bit: the wildflower, Devil's-bit Scabious.

IX *3, May Cottages* (54): *Sirens:* mythical monsters, usually depicted as birds with the faces of women, whose beautiful song lures sailors to their deaths. In *Odyssey* 12, Odysseus, curious to hear their songs for himself, has his men tie him to the ship's mast as they sail past, while plugging their ears with wax.

trad. two-bed cottage: based on Halifax Property Services details.

X *Return to Ithaca* (55): Italic quotation translated from Cavafy's 1894 poem 'Ithaka'.

mother: Odysseus' mother, Anticleia, had died of grief before he reached home – he meets her ghost in the Underworld.

father planting out his grief: during his absence, Odysseus' father, Laertes, kept to his country farm, nursing his grief alone.

wife whose heart unravels: besieged by suitors in his absence, Odysseus' wife, Penelope, devised a scheme tot stall them; promising her admirers that she would chose one of them when she had finished her tapestry, she then unpicked her day's work each night.

dog who's had its day: Odysseus' faithful dog, Argus, dies on his master's return.

lovers' bones: on his return Odysseus kills all the suitors and their accomplices.